The Colour of Canada

The Colour of Canada

with text by
HUGH MacLENNAN

M&S

Contents

McClelland & Stewart Inc.
THE CANADIAN PUBLISHERS
481 University Avenue
Toronto, Ontario
M5G 2E9

Canadian Cataloguing in Publication Data
MacLennan, Hugh, 1907-1990
    The colour of Canada

4th rev. ed.
ISBN 0-7710-5597-8

1. Canada – Description and travel – 1951-1980 – Views.   I. Title.

FC59.M33 1992   971.064'3'0222   C92-093536-2   F1016.M33 1992

PAGE 1: DON RIVER, SERENA GUNDY PARK, TORONTO
PAGE 2: NEAR WATERFORD, NEW BRUNSWICK
PAGE 4-5: TERENCE BAY, HALIFAX COUNTY, NOVA SCOTIA
Endpapers : THE CROWBERRY BUSH GIVES A TOUCH OF
          EVERGREEN TO THE ARCTIC

Prologue

The first edition of this book appeared early in 1967 and was intended as a testimonial to our Centennial Year. We never expected that the demand for it would outlast 1967, but the demand has been constant. These have been long years for all of us, and the psychic and political shiftings both in Canada and in the rest of the world have been dramatic.

How much has happened since that spring afternoon in 1967 when Expo 67 was unveiled in Montreal! Nature itself shone on us that day. The air was crisp, the wind-scoured sky was cloudless, beneath it the St. Lawrence flowed as blue as the Athabasca, and the fields beyond the river were as green as Ireland. On the river islands Expo 67, that perfect melding of French-Canadian flair and Anglo-Canadian practicality, marriage unique between art and technology, seemed to be holding its breath. Here at last was the outward and visible symbol of what Canada could not yet believe she had become.

One by one the flags of the visiting nations rose on their standards in La Place des Nations and were broken free, the name of each of them ringing out like a bell. The whole world seemed to be there. Finally the name "Canada" was spoken, the new Maple Leaf flag went up and instantly a squadron of R.C.A.F. planes cracked over in salute and burst upward like a fan of rockets into the blue.

Up jetted Expo's fountains and I was one of the thousands who felt the lump in the throat. Beside me was my oldest living friend who happened also to be Canada's Auditor-General (he must have spent many a day and night worrying about the cost of all this to the tax-payer) and his eyes suddenly shone. He pounded my back and cried, "My God, we've made it! We've made it after all!"

So indeed it seemed in the halcyon days of May, June and July. So extraordinary was the spirit of Expo that the neighbouring pavilions of Israel and Egypt remained unruffled even during the Six Days' War. Meanwhile all over the land Canadians were celebrating the hundredth birthday of a nation neither the British nor the Americans, nor for that matter too many Canadians themselves, had believed would endure longer than a decade or two. Looking over the national flags assembled there I thought again how ironic history is. Among those 62 visiting nations from all the world's continents only sixteen were politically older than Canada and of these famous veterans, which ones could claim to have been more fortunate?

France was enduring her Second Empire when Canada was born; now she had her Fifth Republic. The Empire on which the sun never set until 1941 had shrunk to the little United Kingdom which soon would abandon nine centuries of stupendously creative isolation and rejoin the continent to which she had originally been attached by Claudius Caesar some two decades after the crucifixion of Christ. The Russia which had been a Czarist agrarian despotism in 1867 was now a communist technological despotism. How many revolutions had Mexico suffered since Canada's birth? How many Greece, Venezuela and Cuba? Austria had shrunk from Europe's greatest land-empire to a tiny state centred on ancient Vienna. Belgium had twice been invaded and occupied; the Netherlands, Denmark, Norway, Greece, Abyssinia and Thailand once invaded and occupied. Japan had convulsed the world, been bombed to the verge of extinction, had recovered astonishingly. Among these politically older

nations, which ones had been so consistently fortunate as ourselves? Only Sweden, Switzerland and the United States.

But even then the tocsins were ringing in Canada and they still are. In 1967 I wrote in the first edition of this book that "I can't give myself the illusion of being sure of many things anymore. Certain facts, knowledges, observations and intuitions – armed and often confused by these, one lives in a world almost but not quite out of human control, its accumulated information so vast that the most learned of men know they are ignorant, its technical communications so efficient that it has been called an electronic village, the new phrase for a technologically created Babel." (Since then Telstar has gone into orbit.) "We try to come to terms with material power such as there never was, matched by an individual uncertainty of soul unparalleled since the Black Death. A new age is a-borning, it is probably here. But nobody I have met or read understands it and not many even pretend to."

Now I must write a strange sentence. We are in the beginning of the first post-Christian Era, yet there are signs everywhere that the spirit of Christ is nearer to men than it has been for centuries.

Also man has made what is probably the most important discovery of his entire career as a species. He has finally found his own true origin. Modern scientific dating applied to a fossil turned up in Africa indicates that we creatures of the big brain, we *homines sapientes sapientes*, have a full-fledged human ancestry which cannot be much older than twenty thousand years. "Wonders are many," sang the chorus in *Antigone*, "but the greatest wonder is man. . . . Cunning beyond fancy's dreams is the fertile skill which brings him, now to evil, now to good."

These lines of Sophocles could serve as a theme song for the years that followed 1967. The great leader who saved France from revolution came to Expo, according to himself with sincere goodwill to all, in order to help a revolution happen here. The Canada which shone so brightly in 1967 sank into the squalid darkness of political kidnapping and murder only three years later. An astounding nexus of technology landed two teams of astronauts on the moon, whence they departed leaving behind them a little plastic *Stars and Stripes* to remind the Creator that Kilroy was there, too. Here on our old earth technology is now admitted, as was not the case in 1967, so to have polluted the air, the waters and the cities that unless it changes its ways it will succeed in collapsing the biosphere. In 1967 Canada wished to recognize Communist China but did not do so for fear of affronting the United States. Five years later Richard Nixon, who had spent a long career denouncing as traitors all who even contemplated a recognition of Mainland China, went to Peking in person and saw to it the whole world watched his performance over television.

We all know that the United States has always been a catalyst in Canadian affairs. Never before have her power-men been so interested in us as they are now. For over a century Canadians have emigrated into the United States and very few Americans settled here. But during the past few years thousands of Americans have been emigrating into Canada and not all of them have come to escape the military draft. Many have come to escape the pollution, and over-crowding, the racial strife and the general over-organization of their native land. But the essential power structure of our neighbour is still in total control and we watch it and wonder what it really intends. We ask ourselves whether sheer pressure of events will compel it to consolidate a kind of Fortress Western Hemisphere in which computer-science will combine with the multi-national American corporations to homogenize the entire New World – as it was called only yesterday before it grew old without ever having really grown up.

If this is to become the policy of the United States, will it mean that Canada is destined to be absorbed and disappear from history at the very moment when she has become mature enough to make an original contribution to it?

Another question-mark. So perhaps this is the time to switch back to the gist of my original text, which may be more urgently applicable to the Canada of now than it was to the Canada of 1967.

Any nation (as distinct from an empire) is ultimately held together by its land, its territory. Most of the pictures in this book are of a Canadian land which is far vaster than any one man can hope to comprehend. It still contains a small nation even though Canada's population today is larger than Britain's in the year of Waterloo. The land will endure as long as the world does, though in what condition will depend upon humanity, yet in the long term the nation is only a tenant on it.

How long the present tenant's lease will run is going to depend upon much more than the nation's present inhabitants. This land is rich and magnificent. After the climate warmed up (lately it is cooling off again) it became much more attractive than it was two centuries ago when Voltaire dismissed it as *quelques arpents de neige.* Everyone knows that the world is now disastrously overcrowded and that the rights of small nations weigh little against hunger, greed, power and the need for living space. However, at the moment the land is still presumed to belong to those who live on it.

In a way, this nation is a miracle of illogicality and nothing is more miraculous about her than her stubborn survival despite the continuous efforts of pundits and businessmen to prove that her survival makes no sense. How often have we heard the reasons – no sense economically, politically, geographically or culturally. She makes no sense, they say. Neither does a giraffe. She is not a logical construction. She never was, and I have the idea that if she ever tries to be logical about herself she will rationalize herself out of existence. As early as 1963, French Canadian separatists had selected the Centennial Year as the logical one for Canada's dissolution. But at the same time Mayor Jean Drapeau went straight ahead and won Expo 67 for Montreal. So it has always been, for political unity as it is understood elsewhere seems the last thing the Canadian people want, though most of them assert that it is our greatest need. Is this logical? Obviously not, and that's fine with me, for if logic is ever carried to its final extreme in human affairs, what does it lead to but insanity? Psychotics are nearly always logical, neurotics never are. But neurotics are at least sane.

"Il est bon," wrote a French philosopher, *"et plus souvent qu'on ne le pense, de savoir de n'avoir pas de l'esprit."* A good thing not to be intelligent? The whole spirit of our century laughs at such an idea. It has bet the bankroll on intelligence. It trusts it so much it has even invented a mechanical brain.

Yet it is a plain fact that many a plain man has been asking for some time what good the super-brains of our century have been doing for humanity. Poor old Einstein's genius led straight to the H-bomb. Hot wars and cold wars, nuclear weapons with miraculous vehicles to deliver them, revolutions and counter-revolutions, rising unemployment combined with rising inflation, laws intended to make us free and secure imprisoning us in strangling bureaucracies, propaganda and Madison Avenue, a super-colossal technology harnessed to produce the one condition of life which man has always found intolerable – leisure. The most brilliant and energetic intellects of our age have occupied themselves with these accomplishments to the virtual exclusion of everything else.

But Canada is not a brilliant nation and one of the few things which seem reasonably clear to me, if to nobody else, is that by pure instinct (there can be no other explanation) we are more strongly than ever asserting the historic decision of our ancestors to stand as aloof as we can from the obsessions and drives of our mighty and (I hope) still friendly neighbour. We have even been saying this publicly lately as hardly any of us did in 1967, but just how aloof we can be is one of those nice calculations so dear to the Canadian soul: all the American investment we can get though not too much American investment; economic union with the United States but not necessarily economic union; all the American university teachers who can't get jobs in their own country must be permitted to take jobs here, but not too many American university teachers; all possible bilingualism and bi-culturalism, but not too much bilingualism and bi-culturism. O Canada, with such subtleties as these we stand on guard for thee!

We all know that the Canadian nation – informal questionnaires put by myself to McGill undergraduates satisfy me that at least 9% of us know it – came into being because our ancestors repudiated the most important single event in the history of the western hemisphere, the American Revolution. Canada exists today because they said no to that. She will cease to exist if she ever says yes to that, unless she does so in the spirit of a girl in the back seat of a taxi with one eye on the meter and the other on the profile of the determined man who took her out that night.

Just the same, that decision of our ancestors has haunted their descendants ever since. The United States has been quite the most marvellous country in the world. She became so rich, successful, exciting and proud, and for years her public pleasure in herself was an enchantment. The ideals on which she was founded rang like bugles around the globe. Her techniques were copied everywhere, and in no countries more meticulously than in Canada and the Soviet Union.

No wonder the descendants of the original Loyalists, looking enviously across the border the British had so negligently agreed to accept for them, asked themselves whether their ancestors had not ruined their children's lives by betting them on the wrong horse. Even some French Canadians thought the same. Calixa Lavalée, the author of our national anthem, was one of them. He left Canada, became an American citizen and from New York sent pamphlets home urging his former countrymen to follow his example. Nor was there ever a lack of those who did. Successive generations were depleted by hundreds of thousands – millions would be no exaggeration – of energetic and able men and women who gravitated like iron filings to the magnet and were lost to Canada.

Nearly everyone called Canada negative in her growing years, and so she was. The only way it seemed possible for French Canada to survive was to make Quebec a virtual reservation, repudiating the value of nearly everything that had happened since 1763. English Canada clung with pathetic loyalty to the fading glories of a Britain that had little interest in her except in time of war or a royal visit. Worse was yet to come. In the twentieth century the final death of the British Empire coincided with the swamping of our information-media by those of the United States, and the old frustration of the baffled horse-player changed into a kind of guilt-neurosis, as though by staying Canadians (and therefore not being Americans) we were defying the will of God. For the Americans were serious when they called the United States "God's Own Country." They still are. "The tremendous prosperity, power and blessing," wrote Billy Graham, "which America has enjoyed through the years came because we as a nation honoured God. It is, I believe, a direct fulfilment of the promise, 'Blessed is the nation whose God is the Lord.'"

But with stubborn negation, often against their conscious minds, the majority of us shied away from Manifest Destiny even after we had been trained to judge our worth solely as we saw it reflected in the eyes of our neighbours. This meant that whenever we boasted about anything, we boasted about our real estate, raw materials, wheat, scenery and Mounted Police, these being the only things Canadian that interested our neighbours. Until, perhaps, recently.

Our destiny, so we were told occasionally by our more optimistic politicians, always lay in some distant future and never was defined. Sir Wilfrid Laurier uttered the famous prediction that just as

the nineteenth century had belonged to the United States, so would the twentieth belong to Canada. Bold statements of this sort are so rare in Canada that this particular one found its way into most of our school books, though anyone who took a good look at it must have known how absurd it was. The nineteenth century never "belonged" to the United States; if it belonged to anyone it belonged to Britain, which cashed in during those years on her victory over France and her headstart in the Industrial Revolution. As for the twentieth century, from 1914 until the first Russian sputnik it clearly "belonged" to the United States, which cashed in on the decline of Europe and her own brilliance in business and technology. But the twentieth century is not over yet. Possibly, though in a sense very different from the one intended by Laurier, at least some of it may be shared by Canada if we have the nerve to follow the instinct of the nation's founders and translate it into a rational purpose.

A nation can become valuable to mankind only if it succeeds in co-operating with what might be called an historical need. For the first time Canada may have a chance of doing that. If we can resolve our own confusions here at home, we will have done more than make Canada a happier and more fruitful country than she is now. We will have set an example to other peoples confused and battered, pulled hither and thither by the struggle and obsessions of the two super-powers.

Let's look backward and ask ourselves frankly what actually were the reasons why the original Canadians repudiated the American Revolution. To understand them might help us make up our minds today. The usual explanations are that the Loyalists were Tories hostile to liberty and progress, while the French Canadian Church abominated democracy worse than the Vatican used to abominate Communism. But surely these explanations are superficial. Why should a French Canada abandoned by such a miserable practicing Catholic as Louis xv, owing neither him nor France an adulterated *sou,* the Union Jack of their conquerors flying over British garrisons in their own cities, have said no to the Americans when they revolted against Britain? The reason was basic; it was not intelligent but visceral. They wanted to survive *as a people*, and it was as simple as that. If they said yes to the Revolution, they would prosper more as individuals in their material lives, but as a people they would disappear and lose all sense of themselves as such.

Why did the Loyalists, most of whom deplored the stupidity and corruption of Lord North's government, refuse to join the Revolution? Certainly not because they were anti-democratic or afraid of losing their privileges. Very few of them were rich and privileged, and if they had been hostile to democracy they never would have introduced the town meeting into Ontario and the Maritime Provinces, nor would their sons have struggled for responsible government in British North America until, without a revolution or severing their ties with the motherland, they won it.

What does all this mean unless it means that what the French Canadians and the Loyalists were rejecting was something deeper than was visible on the surface? Letters and statements made by Loyalists suggest that they knew very well what it was. It was not the ideals of the Revolution, but the hidden passions which those ideals masked.

In a famous book written in 1923 (*Studies in Classic American Literature*) D. H. Lawrence writes with a wild and fascinated eloquence about those drives which lay hidden underneath the idealism of the American Revolution, and few learned Americans have denied that he was basically right, especially in recent years when they have to live with the results of them.

Lawrence sought to explain the startling contradiction between the pride and confidence taken by Americans in their wonderful, rationally created nation and the violence, irrationality and unhappiness that have pervaded most of the best American literature from Melville and Hawthorne until the present day. The typical American hero of the

deepest American literature is nearly always a defeated *individual*, a desperate man alienated from the triumphant crowd: Captain Ahab striking his harpoons into the whale that symbolized the superego of American puritanism and the *Pequod* going down with flag flying, sunk by that same whale which here symbolizes the natural world which the conscious ego had tried to master; the lone American caught by the sheriff's posse and growling, "My name it is Sam Hall and I hate you one and all – God damn your eyes!" and now, in most postwar literature, the defiant American hero has merged into the passive anti-hero who can imagine no other role than civil disobedience. Why all this?

Lawrence finds his explanation in the hidden compulsions of many early New Englanders; had he been more familiar with literature south of the Mason-Dixon Line he would have found examples even more striking. Most of the revolutionary Americans, so Lawrence thought, were seeking to escape, to get away. But from what? The ineffectual authority of an ineffectual king who lived in London? And if there was a determination to create a state where all men would enjoy life, liberty and the pursuit of happiness, why did the revolutionaries retain the institution of slavery? Underneath the perfect rationality of the most perfect constitution lurked something hidden, and it was this that the Loyalists rejected.

Lawrence is right, surely, when he says that what America really sought to escape was nothing less than the human past of Europe – history itself and the long and exhausting burden of it. Under

The South Nahanni River flows almost parallel to the Yukon-Northwest Territories border. Legends telling of rich gold deposits, prehistoric animals and a tropical climate lasted until the river valley was explored in mid-century.

THE GATE, SOUTH NAHANNI, NORTHWEST TERRITORIES

Soft rock formations on the west coast of Hudson Bay are
sculptured and polished by the endless waves and shifting ice.

God in a new continent, they aspired to create a new and purer nation, uncontaminated by the evil past, free forever from the repetitive patterns of history and injustice. "No foreign entanglements" was echoed a century and a quarter later by Henry Ford's "History is bunk."

But nobody can escape from his past, neither can any nation live alone and escape from history, as successive American presidents have discovered. The effort to be superior to the past, superior to human nature, is more than human nature can bear, no matter how nobly people try to bear it. As Lawrence saw it, such an effort was bound to alienate the individual, the blood-and-flesh woman and man, and at the same time exalt and magnify the state which, as its power grew, imperceptibly was given the kind of worship and obedience usually offered to God. "Hear ye, O America, our nation is one nation" – and in order to preserve the mystique of its unity, the most humble and merciful of presidents waged the most terrible civil war in history. Now challenged by a newer messianic ideology, the power and concentration of the state has become . . . but these are deep waters, and we have no fishing rights in them.

But we still do have our huge country and our little nation. Nor is it anti-American to emphasize that it was because Canadians had no wish to alienate themselves from the past and from their European source that the Canadian nation came into being.

Earlier I said that this peculiar nation of ours, in most things important, acts from instinct and sentiment. She has always tried to guard her continuities. If to do so is unfashionable, her leaders pay unfailing lip-service to the pressures of the moment, but in practice they seek to guard the continuities. Why else was there such a soul-searching over the ditching of the Red Ensign in favour of a distinctive national flag? Why else does Quebec insist upon the maintenance of her French culture? Our instinct – perhaps in the insanity of the post-war years our reason goes along with it – tells us now that the only "unity" worth having is one which will permit the greatest possible variety of individual and collective differences, that the individual will have a chance only if he is given priority over the vast, impersonal state. The world today is on a psychic hinge, and the young generation, confused though it is, everywhere recognizes that the challenge it faces in the Age of Affluence is not a material but a spiritual one. Flesh and blood against the abstraction; genuine human needs against the needs of the super-organization.

Therefore I believe that the perennial Canadian "racial" problem is our greatest single asset. Again and again it has prevented us from opting for the kind of unity which turns a government into a huge abstraction. In our own muddled way we are still trying to provide in Canada a political home for diversity. Our two solitudes may still be solitary, but they have begun to talk with one another. Is it still wishful-thinking to believe that if Canada succeeds, she will be a pilot-plant for a broader human liberty in this frightened world? Could anything be worse for the over-burdened United States than to have us inflict our problems upon it?

We still have the land; we are still its tenants. The land is our overwhelming common denominator. A land of dramatic contrasts with an undeveloped frontier – much of it probably undevelopable – almost as large as Europe: great rivers, only a few of them polluted so far; thousands of lakes and three oceans flanking the whole. Stupidly, we overcrowd three urban areas, a buck being still sacred with us. But the plane which leaves Vancouver air terminal flies over virgin mountains within ten or fifteen minutes. The cars streaming out of Montreal and Toronto can usually reach the wilderness in less than two hours. When you stand on a high point in Quebec City you can see only a few miles away the ramparts of the Laurentian Shield.

This land is far more important than we are. To know it is to be young and ancient all at once. Its virginity is our visible link with the beginnings of the race and the millions of New Canadians who

BEARBERRY LEAF IS USED AS TEA, TOBACCO, DYE AND ASTRINGENT.

have come here have found constant reminders of their homes in older countries.

In 1937 when I went through Scandinavia to Russia, I said in Denmark, "But this is like Prince Edward Island"; in Sweden, "How like New Brunswick this is!" In Finland, "Just like Quebec fifteen miles north of the river, or Ontario above Simcoe." In Russia and Poland I though inevitably of the prairie provinces. A few years ago, sailing from Athens along the coast of Argolis, had I not known I was in the Aegean I could easily have mistaken that rocky shore for the coasts of Cape Breton or Newfoundland. British Columbia is our Norway. And one dawn on the Mackenzie, waking in the wheelhouse of a dredge moored at Wrigley Harbour, the sun striking like a searchlight across the river under a mass of clouds, wild ducks and geese arrowing off the water – this was North America when the first white men saw it!

In this book we discover Canada somewhat as the explorers, settlers, and *voyageurs* discovered it. We begin at the rocky harbours of Newfoundland and Nova Scotia, glance at the gentle farmland of Prince Edward Island in summer and winter, at the old Loyalist city of Saint John and some of the lovely rivers of New Brunswick. We come to Gaspé, go up the St. Lawrence past modern Quebec and Montreal, enter briefly the Eastern Townships, then pass through the water gap leading to the Great Lakes and Ontario. We look at the new Toronto and a variety of scenes in Ontario before leaping across the Shield to the Prairies – space apparently limitless under shifting skies all the way to the Rocky Mountains. We go through the mountains to the coast where a sea bird flies out from the land over the Pacific. The North is still a separate region so far as communications and the life of the people are concerned, and we treat it separately in the pictures in this book.

Geographically, Canada consists of five very different regions: first, the Atlantic provinces, glacier-scraped, settled for the most part along the coasts (and in New Brunswick along the rivers), apparently small yet so indented that the coastline of "little" Nova Scotia is some 5,000 miles long – a distance much greater than an air line from Halifax to Victoria; then the nation's core, Quebec-Ontario, bound together despite linguistic differences by the St. Lawrence and Ottawa river systems and the Laurentian Shield; then the Prairies, a sea of land lying between the American border and the arbitrary line of the Northwest Territories; then the Cordilleran West; finally the North. This latter region consists of more than the Yukon, the Northwest Territories and the islands of the Arctic Ocean; along Hudson Strait, Ungava Bay, northern Labrador it overlaps Quebec and Newfoundland.

Canada's geographical vastness is deceptive. At the moment little more than 4% of the whole country is under cultivation; it has been estimated that only 7% ever can be. If the present trend continues, this will become a country where, apart from the Prairies, the population will be congregated in a number of densely populated areas suitable for trade and industry; in short a culture of cities like a colossal ancient Greece, with nature picturesque and largely unspoiled just outside them, a country as different as could be imagined from the United States with its rich parklands and thousands of small market towns.

In 1967, Canadians seemed to welcome this prospect, but now it is beginning to seem somewhat horrible. Now we know at last that urban giantism in some regions of the United States has passed the point of no return. It breeds crime and frustration everywhere and it is no wonder that thousands of Americans in the last few years have been buying Canadian shore and forest land to escape from the concrete jail of modern megalopis. Will Canada move toward decentralization in the next few decades or will her cities develop into a cancer growth? I don't know.

But no matter what the population development, the contrast between the geographical and human maps of Canada will be startling for a long time to come.

OVERLEAF PAGES 18-19: AN INUIT KAYAK, GRISEFIORD,
ELLESMERE ISLAND, N.W.T.

NEAR THE ARCTIC CIRCLE: MIDNIGHT IN MAY

It has often been estimated that by the year 2,000 A.D. the total Canadian population will touch 40 millions, but we make no predictions about that here, remembering that in 1930 the experts predicted that by 1960 the population of the United States would level off at 145 millions. The present population explosion can easily be arrested in the Western nations and already there are indications that a falling-off has begun. Nowhere has this falling-off been more startling than in Quebec. Only twenty years ago the French Canadian birthrate was one of the highest in the western world; today, with the decline in religion, it has shrunk to the lowest in Canada. The only prediction we make here is that the central Mackenzie Basin will be more heavily populated than it is now; the country is beautiful and the mean temperatures in the region of Fort Simpson are higher than they were at Quebec a century ago. If mosquitos and blackflies can be controlled, this would be one of the finest lands anyone could wish.

A culture of cities with unspoiled nature in abundance, more fresh air and water than in any other part of the earth — if only our imaginations could look both back and forward, back to the loveliness of the cities of ancient Greece and forward to what such a combination of urbanity and the wilderness promises us! If only, instead of multiplying urban high rises, our city developers had the wisdom of Sir Christopher Wren, and kept the buildings lower and seeded the cities with parks!

Yet finally, we seem to be saying yes to this land the ancient navigators discovered for us and the *voyageurs* opened up for us. Changes in the climate have made it easier for us than for the pioneers, but it still is a dramatic climate. If it becomes soft and tropical it is never for long. A storm breaks and astringent air pours in from the north to blow away the smog we still believe is allowable because there is temporary profit in it for those who make it. The sky is electric blue and old men remember their youth. This land is too precious to be put at auction.

The Maritimes

ROCKY HARBOUR IN GROS MORNE NATIONAL PARK IN
WESTERN NEWFOUNDLAND

*Look at the art of the sea, how it shapes and polishes granite. Feel its
cold cleanness, its power when it thunders against the land in a whole gale.
On a day like this you can see spume like thin snow rushing across a
rising moor of stunted trees with granite tors standing like prehistoric
monsters. On fine days you can sit here in the sun with your back
propped against North America and your eyes ranging over a sea that
extends uninterrupted to old Guyenne and Gascony.*

OPPOSITE: PEGGY'S COVE, NOVA SCOTIA

22

Poetic names, haunting or majestic, redolent of history: Heart's Content, Seldom-Come-By, Blow-Me-Down, Port-Aux-Basques (here Basque fishermen dried their catches before taking them home), Bonavista Bay, Conception Bay, Placentia Bay, Avalon.

Newfoundland has always been a stepping stone between the hemispheres. Vikings were here before Cabot; Englishmen, Frenchmen, Spaniards, Portuguese shared the fishing rights before the Pilgrims landed in Massachusetts. The Labrador Current washes the island, makes it chilly and foggy; the storms are terrifying. Steamers following the Great Circle from New York to Europe pass in sight of Cape Race, and the Titanic was only the most famous of the ones that failed to finish the voyage. In little boats the fishermen of Newfoundland put out to the rescue in North Atlantic winter gales. Alcock and Brown left Newfoundland in 1919 on the first non-stop trans-Atlantic flight. During World War Two, Gander was the last airport of Ferry Command. Now, after centuries of heroic isolation, Newfoundland is part of Canada, and of the continent, the oldest and newest province.

THE VILLAGE OF BURNT ISLAND ON
THE SOUTH COAST OF NEWFOUNDLAND

TERRA NOVA NATIONAL PARK, NEWFOUNDLAND

St. John's wind-swept, rain-washed houses—warm and comfortable, wonderful houses to grow up in like those of Saint John, N.B. The finest wines in North America are drunk in St. John's. Here, too, is played some of North America's shrewdest politics—politics can only be real where people know each other in the bone and the blood corpuscles, otherwise they are illusions called "images." It was here, too, that Premier Joey Smallwood broke the last family compact in North America.

ST. JOHN'S HARBOUR FROM SIGNAL HILL, NEWFOUNDLAND

The ancient sea still washes the Maritimes, but almost gone is the life when the sea and the small family farms nourished the people. Less than a century ago Maritimers built, sailed and manned one-fifth of the merchant fleets of the entire world. The Cunard and White Star Lines were born here. But modern technology doomed both them and the old life-pattern. Now thousands of shore lots have been bought cheap by foreigners desperate to escape the hideousness that made their cities rich.

INGONISH FERRY, NOVA SCOTIA

In spite of the vagaries of relying on mining and the sea for its day-to-day existence, Nova Scotia still looks back on the grandeur of its long history. The first permanent settlement in Canada was Port Royal, founded by the French in the rich land of the Annapolis Valley in 1605. Over a century later it was renamed Annapolis, in honour of Queen Anne, to celebrate the last of five times the settlement had changed hands between the French and the English. Today the old military buildings nestle amid the green fortifications of Fort Anne.

FORT ANNE, NATIONAL HISTORIC PARK, NOVA SCOTIA

HALIFAX, FOUNDED BY CORNWALLIS IN 1749, IS
ONE OF THE WORLD'S GREAT NATURAL HARBOURS.

The office towers of the new Halifax loom over the historical properties of the
old city. As a Royal Navy base, Halifax knew the admirals from Boscawen
through Nelson to Fisher. The largest Allied convoy base during both World
Wars, Halifax was founded as a base against the French fort of Louisbourg
on Cape Breton Island.

Louisbourg was the loneliest, foggiest, most expensively fortified outpost of any
European power in North America. Garrisoned by French troops, ill-
defended by the French navy, unsupported by such habitant colonists as made
the defence of Quebec an epic, Louisbourg fell to Britain and the New
Englanders in the War of the Austrian Succession, was restored to France
when the war ended, and was refortified at such cost that Louis xv com-
plained that he would soon see the bastions of Louisbourg rising over the
horizon. The city fell for the second and last time in the Seven Years' War,
and this opened Wolfe's way to Quebec. The British razed the city and
fortifications to the ground, and left the site to the fog, the rain, the cold,
and the sea birds.

OPPOSITE: FISHING BOATS, PORT MOUTON, NOVA SCOTIA

OVERLEAF PAGES 32-33: THE GUNS OF THE FORTRESS OF
LOUISBURG

Along the Cabot Trail

No scenic highway in North America compresses into such a short length (188 miles) such an astonishing variety: cliffs, ocean vistas, highland glens, river meadows and a short stretch of the Bras d'Or Lakes. Frigid seas and grayish-pink granite on the Atlantic shore; along the Gulf of St. Lawrence, Sienna-red cliffs and warm water in summer, Mediterranean light on fine days and, from Cap Rouge, a view like the one from Taormina on the eastern coast of Sicily. The people are mostly of Highland Scottish or French ancestry and even now some Gaelic and French lingers.

BESIDE THE CABOT TRAIL, CAPE BRETON ISLAND, NOVA SCOTIA

Not all the Maritimes are stern and rocky. Much of Prince Edward Island is a garden, famous for its potatoes, dairy products, and all that is Anne of Green Gables. It boasts superb Malapeque oysters and seemingly endless miles of sandy beach in Prince Edward Island National Park.

ROCKS AND DUNES AT CAVENDISH BEACH, PRINCE EDWARD ISLAND

The gentle island lies in the path of nor'easters from Labrador bringing blizzards in winter and drift ice in the spring which chokes the harbours. They talk hopefully of a causeway across Northumberland Strait. Will all Cape Breton Island hold enough rock for it?

SUMMERFIELD, PRINCE EDWARD ISLAND

New Brunswick was founded in defiance of the rebels who had triumphed in the new United States, and that Loyalist defiance takes symbolic form on the main street of St. Andrews. The cannon may threaten sea-borne Yankee invaders, and the Union Jack may fly, but American tourists are welcome on the old-fashioned streets of this little town, laid out with care in 1783.

Other Loyalist settlers moved up the St. John river valley, some even ascending beyond the little Acadian fishing village that was transformed into Fredericton. As they moved they brought the distinctive New England style of civilisation, and religion, along with them.

New Brunswick is a land of rivers,
all of them beautiful and none
gigantic. Rich farms and quiet market
towns grew slowly along the banks of
the St. John, Kennebecasis and Peticodiac,
and some of the old houses are jewels.
Fredericton is surely one of the most
dignified little cities in North
America, with an exquisite cathedral
and our oldest university. Until recently,
the St. John was the best salmon river
on the eastern side of the continent.
Dams almost abolished the salmon,
and the great rafts of lumber no longer
come down from northern New Brunswick
and northern Maine to form masses of
bobbing logs several miles square at
Maugerville. Concrete finally destroyed
the river's meaning, but not its beauty.
This was the country where Sir
Charles G. D. Roberts wrote his
nature stories. In the northeast
of the province, the Miramichi
and the Restigouche are famous
salmon streams still.

SAINT JOHN VALLEY, NEW BRUNSWICK

The waterscapes of Nova Scotia

Bridgewater, Nova Scotia

Sand Point Lighthouse, Five Islands, Nova Scotia

Pembroke, Nova Scotia

Blue Rock, Nova Scotia

Port Williams, Nova Scotia

Into Quebec

When national and provincial borders were established in North America at the end of the eighteenth century, the decisive factor was often the movement of flowing water. Madawaska County in northern New Brunswick has a panhandle jutting into Maine because the St. John River flows into the Atlantic. The height of land between New Brunswick and Quebec is shared on the principle that such parts as drain into the Atlantic belong to New Brunswick, while those that drain into the St. Lawrence are in Quebec.

Human flow obeys no such geographic laws. Northern New Brunswick is mostly French speaking today because thousands of French Canadians seeped over the height of land to work in the forests and lumber plants of New Brunswick, or to fish the waters along the shores of the St. Lawrence Gulf. St. Leonard and Edmundston are now as "French" as La Tuque. But along the Gulf Shore, many of the French-speaking New Brunswickers are of the Acadian stock that has been there for centuries.

Northeastern New Brunswick is forest land threaded by famous rivers: the Miramichi, the Restigouche and the Matapedia, which feed millions of logs down to the sawmills and pulp companies at the estuary, and which abounded in salmon until the factory ships discovered the meeting-place of the salmon in the Atlantic and vacuumed up almost nine tenths of them. The Trans-Canada Highway, leaving Edmundston, mounts slowly up past Lake Temiscouta and descends the height of land to reach the St. Lawrence at Rivière du Loup, which looks across to the mountains stretching north-east from Murray Bay. The other road, paralleled by the tracks of the C.N.R., skirts Bay Chaleur with a magnificent view of the Gaspé mountains, then winds through a hundred miles of the Matapedia Valley and reaches the St. Lawrence just below Father Point, where the out-going vessels ship their pilots. Here the St. Lawrence is only nominally a river; it is really a firth of the sea — salt water deep enough to enable German submarines to operate in it during 1942, cold winds from the icebergs trapped in Belle Isle, and sometimes schools of white porpoises playing about the cutwaters of hurrying ships.

THE MILL AT SAINT-ETIENNE-DE-BEAUMONT, QUEBEC

Opposite Percé Rock Jacques Cartier is said to have landed for the first time on what is now Canadian soil. Here, too, Bishop Laval celebrated his first Canadian Mass, in 1659. The arch in the fifteen-hundred-foot rock is sixty feet high. A few miles seaward is the bird sanctuary of Bonaventure Island —a colony of gulls, cormorants, gannets and puffins that dive for fish in the frigid waters of the Gulf of St. Lawrence.

PERCÉ ROCK, GASPÉ, QUEBEC

The village of Tadoussac looks out on one of the world's unique spectacles – the St. Lawrence estuary, deep enough to have hidden German submarines in the war and salty enough for schools of white porpoises. What Cartier mistook for the Northwest Passage became the cradle of Canada and a water route into America's heart. Now the Seaway leads ships of the world to the Great Lake ports; also lamprey eels, which destroy the

*wonderful Great Lakes fish. The Seaway also tempted
Montreal union leaders to make their port so costly
that Halifax has gained more trade than she feared she
would lose when the Seaway was originally proposed.*

ALONG THE ST. LAWRENCE RIVER, TADOUSSAC, QUEBEC

The cradle of Canada, Quebec has always been close to history's heart

Quebec stands at the confluence of the St. Charles and St. Lawrence rivers. Lower Town is on the waterfront, while Upper Town is built on Cape Diamond, rising above the river. The site of Quebec was first visited by Cartier in 1535; Champlain established the city in 1608, twenty-two years before Boston was founded. Subsequently, both New France and the fur trade were governed from Quebec. Throughout its history, epochal events have centred on men who were associated with her: Frontenac, Laval, Montcalm, Wolfe, Dorchester, Benedict Arnold, and Nelson. Here, in 1943, Winston Churchill and Franklin Roosevelt, with their generals, admirals and airmen, made the final plans for the Normandy Invasion of June 6, 1944.

THE CHATEAU FRONTENAC FROM
LOWER TOWN, QUEBEC CITY

QUÉBEC CITY, QUEBEC

The many battles for Quebec had an ironic final outcome. The British took the city from the French in order to ensure a safe water route to the Ohio Valley for their American colonists. But the newly secured northern boundary only made it easier for the Americans to rebel against the British. In 1783, when the Treaty of Versailles acknowledged that it was all over, the British still held Quebec, but the Americans owned the United States.

A WINTER EVENING ON ONE OF THE NARROW STREETS OF
OLD QUEBEC CITY

THE OLYMPIC STADIUM, MONTREAL

Montreal, French by birth and now, after the efforts of the Parti Québécois, again French in spirit. An Empire city (though without an Empire) because of its location at one of the strategic points of commerce and of the movements of people. Violently dramatic in climate, Montreal can be hotter than Singapore and as cold as the Arctic, as smoggy as London used to be and electrically vibrant with glittering skies when the northern weather fronts assert themselves. If its crime rate reminds one of Chicago's, it remains a city of bells, from which the Angelus rings as in the Middle Ages. Described half a century ago as "an English garrison surrounded by a French village," it is now a thoroughly French metropolis, a seaport with ski slopes an hour from its skyscrapers.

MONTREAL, QUEBEC

Montreal — A little old world magic in the middle of North America

Cities are like water: they seek their own levels. If located on plains, they spread formlessly like water in a marsh. If constrained by nature or walls, they concentrate their forces into a tension at the core. Montreal lies on an island in a river with a mountain in its centre, so her core is concentrated.

Here are the old, the new, the powerful, the helpless, the chic and the chi-chi, reality and illusion for a precarious moment linked in a bizarre harmony, ugliness not yet triumphant, ordinariness threatening everywhere but still held in check.

This column to Horatio Lord Nelson, situated just above Place Jacques Cartier, is older than the one in London's Trafalgar Square.

Victorian gingerbread architecture — fills every inch of space with porches, railings, domes, and cupolas.

Classic transition: Upper-middle-class mansion to lower-class rooming house to everyone's-class "maison de rendezvous" — "a boutique".

The glass mountain range of the Banque Nationale de Paris building on McGill Avenue reflects the modern city-scape of downtown Montreal.

A snow-covered staircase winds grace-fully downward — bearing a single set of footprints to the road below.

Local quarries provided the grey limestone used in many buildings until the turn of the century.

Twin staircases seem to lean against each other in an attitude of perfect indifference and privacy.

On the side streets of old Montreal, worn cobblestones wind down to the harbour, providing a perfect contrast to the glass and steel of the new construction in the downtown area. The charm of eating in a three hundred year old building never fails to attract tourists.

Plunging three stories in the
concourse of Montreal's giant
Stock Exchange, a sculptured glass
chandelier sheds a new light on
the business of an old city.

PLACE VICTORIA, MONTREAL, QUEBEC

Notre Dame in Montreal was for many
years the largest church north of Mexico.
With its impressive size, its twin
towers, and its Gothic decoration,
it closely resembles the cathedral of
the same name in Paris, France.

NOTRE DAME,
MONTREAL, QUEBEC

It has been said that Quebec's
Eastern Townships remind
everyone of some other place
they know and love. This
region was originally marked out
by Lord Dorchester as land
for Loyalists from New England.
The descendants of the old
settlers still speak in Yankee
twangs, but now the region
is predominately French-speaking
as French Canadians have
moved in from more crowded areas
to farm the land. Hence
some of the place names: Saint-
Adolfe de Dudswell, St. Paul
d'Abbotsford, Stukely Sud and
Ham Sud. Americans have
called the Townships "a
geographical extension
of New England" — it depends upon
the point of view. There are
splendid lakes like Massawippi,
Memphremagog, Orford.
Hills like the one here, very many
of them, almost but not
quite mountains, loom over the
pasture lands and farms
and in the autumn they blaze or
glow with the scarlet of
maples, the yellow of birches,
the copper of oaks, the
pastel russet-red of butternuts.
The St. Francis is the
principal river and on its banks
is the third largest city
in Quebec. Sherbrooke, once
centred on an English
garrison (when Lord Palmerston
became Colonial Secretary
his first order was to strengthen
it against a possible
American invasion) is now largely
French-speaking.

THE IRON HILL ROAD, IRON HILL,
QUEBEC

SUGARLOAF, MONTMORENCY FALLS, QUEBEC

Montmorency Falls was named by Champlain in honour of the Duc
de Montmorency, who was the Viceroy of New France between 1619
and 1624. Today, a hydro-electric power plant harnesses the rush of
the water over the falls, but they are not yet tamed. In winter, the
falls provide dangerous recreation: the almost perpendicular walls of
ice challenge the nerves and stamina of glacier climbers.

Up in the Laurentians

The Laurentians are best in winter,
and in Montreal "going north"
means "going ski-ing."
But before the ski-ing, French
Canadians hacked farms
out of the rare patches of arable land
in this Shield country
and built their parishes, with
simple churches like this
one in St. Faustin.

Ontario

There is no dramatic geographic division between Quebec and Ontario because both provinces are dominated by the St. Lawrence River system and the Laurentian Shield. Along and above the shores of lakes Ontario and Erie, in the Niagara Peninsula and in the larger peninsula terminating at the Detroit and St. Clair rivers, the Ontario land is much richer than the land in Quebec and more extensively farmed: hence the greater number of small towns and cities. But farther north the shield country is much the same in both provinces.

The real division is ethnic and historical, Quebec having been settled by French-speaking Roman Catholics, Ontario by Protestant Loyalists later reinforced by Protestant Scots and Irish, with the consequence that for a long time Europe's old religious rivalries continued in Canada. This particular outlet for human stupidity is now far less important than it was. "French" and "English" may still be two solitudes, but at least they are learning to respect each other. Their joint ownership of the land makes this necessary, just as, a century ago, it made it necessary for them to form a political union. They knew that if they could not hang together, they would hang separately.

Ontario

Ottawa was the most unlikely spot anyone could imagine for a national capital. A century ago it was an over-grown lumber village noted for its drunken brawls and cholera epidemics. The decision to make it the capital of the new nation was made for the reason that most important Canadian decisions are made: no other choice seemed possible. Kingston was too close to the American border, which then was not unfortified. Montreal was too "French"; Toronto too "English". Ottawa had twin advantages: the Rideau Canal linked it to Kingston; the river to Montreal and the St. Lawrence.

Though Ottawa still has a few surviving relics of its unsightly past, some of it now is beautiful. The National Capital Commission's labours come to slow fruition in public gardens and landscaped parks. Lumbermen have given way to civil servants. The embassies of the world's nations are here. The tensions of a tense world are expressed here in the guarded understatements of men who know that lives and fortunes can hang on the words they use.

PARLIAMENT BUILDINGS,
OTTAWA, ONTARIO

Toronto is a textbook example of urban renewal. Huge office towers, dozens of theatres, more movie-goers per capita than any other city, mazes of shopping malls, restaurants, and safe streets make the city core a playground for those who can afford to live there, and for the growing numbers of tourists and convention-goers who visit the city every year. Resented for its power and supposed smugness, and laughed at for being so clean, Toronto is exciting, except for the poor, who are being forced out of the high-priced downtown into the suburbs in order to find affordable housing.

THE CN TOWER AND THE HARBOURFRONT ANTIQUE MARKET, TORONTO

OPPOSITE: CHRISTMAS IN THE EATON CENTRE, TORONTO

If a Torontonian who had died
in 1967 could return to life, he
could not believe this scene in Yorkville.
This district, two blocks north of Bloor
Street, was once a residential area.
Then, in the sixties, it became the
Greenwich Village of Toronto.
Now the houses have been turned into
smart boutiques and art galleries.

The great shift in Canadian
morals and mores which began
after the Hitler War is more obvious
in Toronto even than in Montreal.
The traditional puritanism has
cracked wide open – with mixed results.
The New Canadians may turn out
to be the catalytic agents who will
direct this new-found energy
into creative channels. Canada was
luckier than the United States
in the time at which she received the
human flood from the European continent. The New Canadians who
came here after the Hitler
War, even the working classes, were
educated men and women, the
beneficiaries of the educational
reforms introduced into their native
lands in the twentieth century.

YORKVILLE AVENUE,
TORONTO, ONTARIO

71

Ontario Place was the first part of an entire new lakefront development program for Toronto.

ONTARIO PLACE, TORONTO, ONTARIO

OPPOSITE: CITY HALL, TORONTO, ONTARIO

Ontarians are really the most
astonishing people in Canada.
Stratford, for years dependent on
its locomotive factories, its
most famous citizen the hockey player
Howie Morenz, as the result of a
dream in the mind of Tom Patterson,
the genius of Sir Tyrone Guthrie
and the unlocked talents of Canadian
actors from all over the country,
is now the Shakespearean centre of the
continent, with thousands of
people coming from everywhere each
summer season to see the plays
as the Elizabethans saw them. One
leaves the theatre after the
evening performance. The sky is clear,
the people move slowly, the waters
of the Avon reflect the lights:

    Look, how the floor of heaven
Is thick inlaid with patines of
      bright gold:
There's not the smallest orb which
      thou behold'st
But in his motion like an angel
      sings...

SHAKESPEAREAN FESTIVAL THEATRE,
STRATFORD, ONTARIO

"And Niagara stuns with thundering sound"...
Goldsmith, who had never seen the Falls, imagined them
in 1770 as one of the horrors awaiting the poor folk expelled from
The Deserted Village in the time of the British enclosures.
History, the eternal ironist!

To Canadians from the Maritimes,
Quebec and the Prairies, the
farmland of Ontario seems almost
too good to be true. It is
gentle, rich and rolling, well
watered, soothed by mists
and moisture from the Great Lakes.
In winter it seems asleep,
but rarely are the winters harsh
enough to kill plants. From
thousands of family farms like these
came the young men and women who
fed the province's famous universities.
Conservative as farm-bred people
always are — they know that nature
cannot be rushed and that
forced plants are weak plants — they
have always balanced the restless
drive and change of Toronto,
which may be the provincial capital
but does not yet control the
provincial legislature.

OPPOSITE: HOCKLEY VALLEY, ONTARIO

OPPOSITE: NEAR DORCHESTER,
ONTARIO

The North begins in Ontario at
Georgian Bay, but in summer
it's warm enough for rattlesnakes.
Naked rock formations stand
magnificent against the sky and in
the tremendous autumn storms
the blowing maple leaves stain
the air. It was here that
Tom Thomson and his colleagues of
the Group of Seven first
painted the Canadian northland
as it truly is, and thereby
enabled millions of their countrymen
to see the nature of their land.

GEORGIAN BAY, ONTARIO

Scattered along a fifty-mile stretch of
the St. Lawrence River, the Thousand
Islands are among the oldest and most
popular vacation centres in northeastern
North America. The U.S.–Canadian
border passes among them, and the
islands themselves, composed of Pre-
cambrian rock, are remnants of the axis
that once linked the Canadian Shield
with the Adirondacks of New York
State. The Indians called them Mana-
toana, "the garden of the Great Spirit."
Today the islands, and other areas
within reach of Ontario's cities, provide
moments of peace and beauty for many.

THOUSAND ISLANDS, ONTARIO

Vignettes of Ontario:

*Patterns of leaves and trees; icicles and plenty—
Ontario's wealth is found in the city but much of
her spiritual beauty rests in the carefully tended
countryside; the Gardiner Expressway,
Toronto — Scarborough Bluffs, near Toronto.*

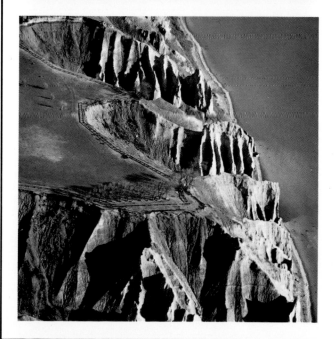

The Prairies

From Ottawa to the Prairies along the line of the Canadian Pacific you travel for a night, a day and most of the night following and nearly all of this journey is through the empty land of the Shield, the train wiggling like a mechanical snake around little lakes, with aspens and spruce blurring past the windows. Before sunset in summer you reach Lake Superior and it is like coming upon an ocean. Port Arthur and Fort William, now united under the tremendous name of Thunder Bay...then into the Shield again and at dawn you are at Kenora and the Lake-of-the-Woods. Living in a few hours through that appalling terrain, you may think back and try to imagine the miracle of the voyageurs who reached Fort William, birchbark canoes, four tons of trade goods and thirty-six portages, thirty-six to forty days after leaving Montreal.

Then the rocks thin out. Suddenly you see black earth appearing and then you are in a land-ocean, the black prairie of Manitoba, on the horizon is a grain elevator and the onion dome of a Ukrainian church.

The breaching of the frontier between Ontario and the West is still the greatest achievement in the history of Canada. In this age of masses and abstractions, let it not be forgotten that this was the work of a very few men, that guts and imagination working together are the expression of the Divine in human life.

THE GARDINER DAM HOLDS BACK WATER TO FORM
LAKE DIEFENBAKER, SOUTH SASKATCHEWAN RIVER,
SASKATCHEWAN

FARMING IN THE QU'APPELLE VALLEY, SASKATCHEWAN

The towns with their grain elevators are like ships
in this land-sea. Also, just as at sea, the weather dominates.
The movement of clouds, their rapid changes of colour,
make the wind visible. When the wheat is ripe, it writhes in
the wind, it boils in the wind, ominously gold under the
darkened sky, Van Gogh's wheatfield near Arles on a colossal scale.

MAIDSTONE, SASKATCHEWAN

Who Has Seen The Wind—
the verb is the decisive word in
the title of W. O. Mitchell's
wonderful novel of a boy
growing up on the prairie, discovering
life, love, cruelty, fear
and God in the movement of grain,
in the sound of the wind,
in the prairie birds and animals.
A land which might have produced
Hebraic prophets looking up
to that appalling sky and asking
the Creator, ''What is man,
that thou art mindful of him'' and
more than once coming to the
conclusion that He is not. Mitchell's
phrase that here life is reduced
to ''the common denominator of sky and
Saskatchewan prairie'' serves
better than reams of analysis to
explain the feeling of prairie
people that their life is unique,
that the people in the East
and on the Pacific Coast can never
really understand them.
It explains the almost perpetual
political opposition of the
prairie provinces to whatever is the
ruling party in the central
Canadian government.

ABOVE: STORM SKY, THE PRAIRIES;

RIGHT: WHEAT AT HARVEST

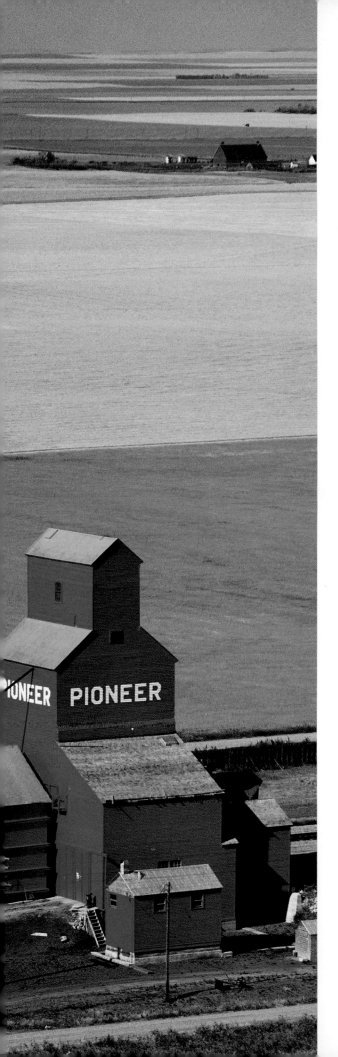

Bleak – yes. Yet, so mysterious is beauty, haunting.
The stark word PIONEER is still apt
on this grain elevator on a siding of the trans-
continental railway line which links it to
Montreal and Vancouver. On these plains when
the first settlers came in, the creak of
the wooden wheels in the Red River carts sounded
for miles; then came the lonely wail of the
whistles on the steam locomotives; now, there's the
penetrating blare of the new horns on the Diesels.

ABOVE: HORSES GRAZE THE WESTERN PASTURE

LEFT: ELEVATORS AT GRAND COULEE, SASKATCHEWAN

93

ABOVE: MUTTART CONSERVATORY, EDMONTON

OPPOSITE: THE CANADIAN MINT, WINNIPEG

Apart from the Red River Settlement, out of which Fort Garry grew into Winnipeg, all of the development of the Prairies began after Confederation. The unarticulated courage of these early pioneers can hardly be comprehended even with the imagination. They came from Europe and the East—came out to a land without trees, and therefore without the wood to build shelters. Thousands of them began their new lives in sod huts, just as the Russians did long ago in the steppes. Today they are raising hills on the prairie. They have even made a good attempt to defeat the climate, at least in one dazzling part of Edmonton, where you can view plant displays, including those from tropical, arid and temperate climates, in the four pyramid-shaped pavilions of the striking Muttart Conservatory.

Edmonton, Calgary, Regina—prairie cities where the land is flat and the winter temperatures dip to fifty below. It is in the cities that you realize what the people have done in such a short time. Today, oil has transformed the look of Calgary and Edmonton with huge office towers and signs of conspicuous wealth: restaurants, theatres, and even art galleries from Toronto are learning to cater to the new cultural consciousness of the West.

THE LEGISLATIVE BUILDING, REGINA, SASKATCHEWAN

OPPOSITE TOP: THE CALGARY SKYLINE

OPPOSITE BOTTOM: EDMONTON CONVENTION CENTRE AND
CANADA PLACE, ALBERTA

Banff National Park preserves 2,564 square miles of breathtaking scenery and is the oldest and most popular of Canada's national parks. Jasper National Park, one of the largest parks on the continent, extends along the eastern slope of the Canadian Rockies in the western part of Alberta, with Banff National Park joining its boundary to the south and Mount Robson Provincial Park in British Columbia adjoining it to the west.

ABOVE: ICEFIELD PARKWAY, WITH CROWFOOT GLACIER, BANFF NATIONAL PARK, ALBERTA

OPPOSITE: PULPIT PEAK, HECTOR LAKE, BANFF NATIONAL PARK

BELOW: SKIING IN THE ROCKIES

When you travel across the far western prairie, the dramatic moment comes, not when you see the skyline of the Rockies, but when you reach the visible tilt where the prairie begins to rise. The foothills begin, rolling like the smaller waves that herald the titanic seas of a hurricane.

MEADOW, BOW LAKE, ALBERTA

These badlands look as if the producer of an epic Western hired Salvador Dali to design the sets. The Hoodoos seem to undulate, almost to breathe; so it is no surprise that people have always searched here for the dinosaur remains that would prove the badlands were once alive.

THE HOODOOS, ALBERTA

British Columbia

The natural division between the Prairies and the cordilleran West is the most dramatic of them all. The Great Divide in the so-called Canadian Rockies marks the line of demarcation between Alberta and British Columbia. This is the range of mountains that separates the waters flowing easterly to reach the Atlantic through Hudson Bay, and westerly to reach the Pacific. In the case of the Peace and Athabasca rivers, the waters drain through the Mackenzie Basin to the Arctic. The Columbia Icefield, straddling the divide, is the source of major rivers that reach all three oceans.

The piercing of the vast ranges of the British Columbia mountains by the railways was Canada's greatest single response to the physical challenge of her environment. The success of Confederation depended upon it. In our time, the bulldozer has enabled the magnificently scenic Trans-Canada Highway to make it possible for automobiles to pass through the ranges on comfortable grades all the way to the coast.

Among the wisest acts ever performed by federal parliament were the ones that created the national parks — Waterton Lakes (which is part of the International Peace Park straddling the U.S. border), Banff, Yoho, Jasper, Kootenay, and others. Though Banff and Jasper are technically in Alberta, they belong to the cordilleran region of the Canadian West. Here, if nowhere else on this progressive continent, the balance of nature still holds. Elk, moose, deer, antelope, bears black and grizzly, marmots and other rodents, even wolves live without fear of the hunter, and anyone can see them who visits the parks.

The prairie begins its transformation into foothill and then to mountain once you have passed the 110th meridian of longitude. Farther south, in Colorado, the moment arrives some eight meridians of longitude farther east, the Canadian prairie being wider than the American because the Rockies swerve easterly south of the border. After the swells of the foothills come the waves of the Rockies, grey, minaretted, the earth in tempest all the way to the Pacific. Yet, in the troughs of these waves are the absolute stillness of the valleys and the perfect reflection of the mighty rocks in placid, glacier-fed lakes.

YOHO NATIONAL PARK, LOOKING DOWN ON MARY LAKE FROM MT. SCHAFFER, B.C.

MOUNTAIN MEADOWS, MT. REVELSTOKE, B.C.

British Columbia's rivers are the most spectacular
on the continent. The incredible Fraser, charging down
the Rocky Mountain Trench, bending around
the Cariboo, confined in its canyon all the way down
to Hope, passing tranquilly through the nation's
most beautiful farmed valley into its delta, issuing in
the Georgia Strait, is as long as the Rhine and is
the greatest salmon breeder in the world. Here we see
the Thompson, named after the geographer of
the North West Company. At Lytton it smashes into the Fraser
like a liquid battering ram, blue water sharp
against the Fraser's brown, then is swallowed and disappears.

TOP: C.N. RAIL LINE ALONG THOMPSON RIVER, BRITISH
COLUMBIA

The Kootenay, four hundred miles long,
rises in the B.C. Rockies, flows south into Montana and
Idaho, then bends north and returns to Canada
to enter Kootenay Lake, a lake seventy-five miles long,
so magnificent that the only word fit to describe
it is its own name. Leaving the lake, it discharges into
the Columbia, which flows south across the American border.
The character of these mountain rivers is schizophrenic:
where the drop is rapid and they are confined, they are raging
torrents of incalculable power; wherever the flow slackens, they
are tranquil vistas of water reflecting the sky.

BOTTOM: FERTILE FLATS OF THE KOOTENAY RIVER, CRESTON,
BRITISH COLUMBIA

ABOVE: RAIN FOREST, VANCOUVER ISLAND

OPPOSITE: TOTEM POLES AT STANLEY PARK, VANCOUVER

Civilization in its early stages resulted from inertia: the invention of agriculture stopped nomadic habits and pinned the people long enough in one place to enable them to foster crafts and arts. On the British Columbia coast the abundance of salmon played this role. It held the people to the river mouths. When Alexander Mackenzie encountered the Indians of the coast he marvelled at their art, but even more did he marvel at their skill with canoes. He said they were superior to his own voyageurs, the ultimate accolade.

The Douglas firs of British Columbia, some of them, are more than a thousand years old. In the Redpath Museum of McGill University is a cross section of one of them, its inner rings indicating its age. When it first began to grow, Alfred the Great was King of England.

IRRIGATED VINEYARDS ALONG SIMILKAMEEN RIVER,
LOWER OKANAGAN VALLEY

Unlike the huge tracts of land needed to raise cattle profitably, many of the Okanagan fruit farms are less than fifty acres, and still provide a decent living for the farmer and his family. But here, like in the rest of Canada, even in tough economic times it is not easy to find the farm labourers willing to do the exhausting physical labour of harvesting.

Vancouver, the western terminus of the railway lines that made Canada a nation, on the sheltered waters of the Georgia Strait, its site discovered in the eighteenth century by the British naval explorer Captain George Vancouver, has the most enviable future of any city in Canada. It has grown with astonishing speed from a small lumber town into Canada's third-largest city.

VANCOUVER'S WATERFRONT

Here the engineers and planners have not failed. The Lions Gate Bridge perfectly combines utility with art, which always conspires with nature. At night, in fog, or in sun, this bridge never lets its setting down. It never seeks to impose itself upon its surroundings. It becomes part of them, and by so doing, helps to define them.

LIONS GATE BRIDGE, VANCOUVER, BRITISH COLUMBIA

THE PAVILION, STANLEY PARK, VANCOUVER, BRITISH COLUMBIA

Stanley Park has an aquarium, a small zoo with native animals and reptiles, gardens, flowering shrubs, and giant trees. Salt water laps its shores; in fog it is mysterious; in fine weather, the sun filters through the branches of the trees. But the mood of the park is natural, and what men have done to improve it does not intrude on its wonderful natural setting. It is a pleasant thought that the seaward tip of Canada's Atlantic port, Halifax, is also a natural park, though there the trees are nearly all spruce and pines, and in winter it's cold. It never seems cold in Stanley Park. The air is as soft as it is in Cornwall, and the climate is similar.

QUEEN ELIZABETH CONSERVATORY, VANCOUVER, BRITISH COLUMBIA

116

The sheltered waters of Georgia Strait, with Vancouver Island acting as a giant breakwater, are almost perfect for yachting and small-boat cruising. In the outer harbour, children can learn to sail in dinghies. Larger craft have the prospect of the entire coast of British Columbia.

YACHT CLUB, WEST VANCOUVER, BRITISH COLUMBIA
OPPOSITE: IN VANCOUVER HARBOUR, BRITISH COLUMBIA

OVERLEAF: LONG BEACH, PACIFIC RIM NATIONAL PARK, BRITISH COLUMBIA

Victoria, capital of British
Columbia, was founded in
1843 as a Hudson's Bay Company's
trading post known as
Fort Camosun, later renamed
Victoria in honour of
the Queen. Its suburb, Esquimalt,
is the western base of the
Canadian Navy. It became the capital
of the province in 1866,
is the western base of the
Confederation and five years before
British Columbia joined Canada
as the sixth province (one year after
Manitoba). When we remember
that, in 1870, Victoria was divided
from "Canada" by more than
two thousand miles of Shield country,
prairies almost empty of
humanity, by hundreds of miles of
mountains, the boldness of
this decision takes the breath away.
As a Canadian newspaper
recently pointed out, if computers had
existed a century ago such a decision
would never have been made.
All the evidence that men could
have fed into it would have
said "no" to it . . .

OPPOSITE:

PARLIAMENT BUILDINGS,

VICTORIA, BRITISH COLUMBIA

RIGHT:

ENGLISH BAY

The cameras have come to the end of a journey that began in Newfoundland and ended in Vancouver Island. They have tried to follow the long thread of settlement from coast to coast. They have omitted most of Canada; how could they possibly have included more than a minuscule suggestion of the enormous land?

We live in a world so filled by the inspirational messages of professional phrase-makers, commercial and political, that we have bred a generation whose ears are sealed to the truth even if the truth is optimistic. We live in a world so stupefied and confused by scientific surveys, opinion polls, computerized predictions that most of us for the sake of our sanity make our separate peace pacts with these insensate abstractions. In Canada we are still asking ourselves the question, "Who are we?" It would be better to look at what we are and what the nation has done in so short a time.

In the funeral oration delivered by Pericles to the Athenians more than four hundred years before Christ, he made the classic understatement. "Our city is superior to the report of her."

Canada would not look like much if she were merely superior to the report of her given by a lot of her citizens. The fact is that her record is almost incredible. Now, after a long winter of subterranean growth, her artists and writers, musicians and dancers are beginning to express her meaning not only to their own people, but to the outside world. She is joining articulate civilization and is earning her right to do so.

Hugh MacLennan

1907-1990

The author of this book was one of Canada's most distinguished novelists. Born in Nova Scotia, he won a Rhodes scholarship and studied at Oxford and, later, at Princeton, before publishing his first novel, Barometer Rising, in 1941. His great contribution to Canadian literature was recognized by the many honorary degrees he received, and his work was translated into many languages. A fellow of the Royal Society of Canada and of the Royal Society of Literature (London), he won Governor General's awards for his novels Two Solitudes, The Precipice and The Watch That Ends The Night, and for two volumes of essays. In 1967 he was made a Companion of the Order of Canada, and in 1980 published his last novel Voices in Time. His work is anthologised in the 1991 book Hugh MacLennan's Best.

Photo Credits

Credits are listed by page numbers.
All Masterfile photos are copyright
by the photographer.

1	George Hunter	57	Barbara K. Deans TOP LEFT AND RIGHT	98	E. Otto/Miller Comstock TOP
2	E. Otto/Miller Comstock		Derek Caron/Masterfile TOP MIDDLE	98-99	E. Otto/Miller Comstock
4-5	George Hunter/Masterfile		E. Otto/Miller Comstock BOTTOM	100	Sherman Hines/Masterfile
13	Stephen J. Krasemann/Masterfile	58	Eberhard E. Otto/Miller Services	101	Sherman Hines/Masterfile
14	Doug Wilkinson	59	John de Visser	104-105	George Hunter/Masterfile
16	Karl Sommerer/Miller Comstock	60-61	E. Otto/Miller Comstock	106-107	Eberhard E. Otto/Miller Services
18-19	Sim 2/Miller Comstock	62	Mia and Klaus	108-109	George Hunter/Miller Comstock BOTH
20-21	Doug Wilkinson	63	Malak/Miller Comstock ALL	110	Paul Baich
22	Michael Saunders/Miller Comstock	66-67	George Hunter/Masterfile	111	Bob Chambers/Miller Comstock
23	Sherman Hines/Masterfile	68	R. Hall/Miller Comstock	112-113	George Hunter/Miller Comstock
24-25	R. Hall/Miller Comstock	69	John Foster/Masterfile	114	Malak/Miller Comstock
26	John de Visser/Masterfile	70-71	Alan Jones/Miller Comstock	115	George Hunter/Miller Comstock
26-27	J. Jacquemain/Miller Comstock	72	George Hunter/Miller Comstock	116-117	George Hunter/Miller Comstock
28	Eberhard E. Otto/Miller Services	73	W. Griebeling/Miller Comstock	118-119	Bob Chambers/Miller Comstock
29	R. Hall/Miller Comstock	74-75	R. Hall/Miller Comstock	120	Jack Long
30-31	E. Hayes/Miller Comstock	76-77	E. Otto/Miller Comstock	121	Miller Comstock
31	Miller Comstock	78	E. Otto BOTH	122-123	E. Hayes/Miller Comstock
32-33	E. Otto/Miller Comstock	79	J. Jacquemain/Miller Comstock	124	Larry J. MacDougal/Miller Comstock
34-35	Steve Vidler/Miller Comstock	80-81	Ted Grant/Masterfile	125	Kenji Nagai/Miller Comstock
36	E. Otto/Miller Comstock	82	Barbara K. Deans/Masterfile TOP LEFT	127	Gerald Campbell
37	Bob Brooks		Peter Varley MIDDLE LEFT	Endpapers	Karl Sommerer/Miller Comstock
38	Michael Saunders/Miller Comstock		John de Visser TOP AND MIDDLE RIGHT		
39	George Hunter/Miller Comstock		Freeman Patterson/Masterfile BOTTOM RIGHT		
40-41	Malak/Miller Comstock	83	Barbara K. Deans TOP LEFT		
42	Bob Brooks		John de Visser OTHERS		
43	Eric Hayes/Miller Comstock TOP LEFT	86-87	George Hunter/Miller Comstock		
43	Bob Brooks	88	Malak/Miller Comstock		
46	Karl Sommerer/Miller Comstock	89	E. Otto/Miller Comstock		
47	Mia and Klaus	90	Horst Ericht		
48-49	Karl Sommerer/Miller Comstock	91	Malak		
50-51	Ted Grant/Masterfile	92-93	George Hunter/Miller Comstock		
52	E. Otto/Miller Comstock	93	Miller Comstock		
53	Miller Comstock	94	E. Otto/Miller Comstock		
54	E. Otto/Miller Comstock	95	George Hunter/Miller Comstock		
55	Miller Comstock	96	Larry J. MacDougal/Miller Comstock TOP		
56	Sam Tata TOP		E. Otto/Miller Comstock BOTTOM		
	WF 1984 Miller Comstock BOTTOM RIGHT	97	W. Griebeling/Miller Comstock		
	John de Visser OTHERS